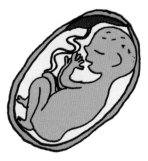

This edition first published in 2020 by Gecko Press
PO Box 9335, Wellington 6141, New Zealand
info@geckopress.com

English-language edition © Gecko Press Ltd 2020
Translation © Don Bartlett 2020

Original title *Hvordan lager man en baby?* © Cappelen Damm AS 2019

Distributed in the United States and Canada by Lerner Publishing Group, lernerbooks.com
Distributed in the United Kingdom by Bounce Sales and Marketing, bouncemarketing.co.uk
Distributed in Australia and New Zealand by Walker Books Australia, walkerbooks.com.au

This translation has been published with the financial support of NORLA.

NORLA
NORWEGIAN LITERATURE ABROAD

Edited by Penelope Todd
Typesetting by Carolyn Lewis
Printed in China by Everbest Printing Co. Ltd, an accredited ISO 14001 & FSC-certified printer

ISBN: 978-1-776572-85-4

For more curiously good books, visit geckopress.com

ANNA FISKE

HOW DO YOU MAKE A BABY?

Translated by Don Bartlett

GECKO PRESS

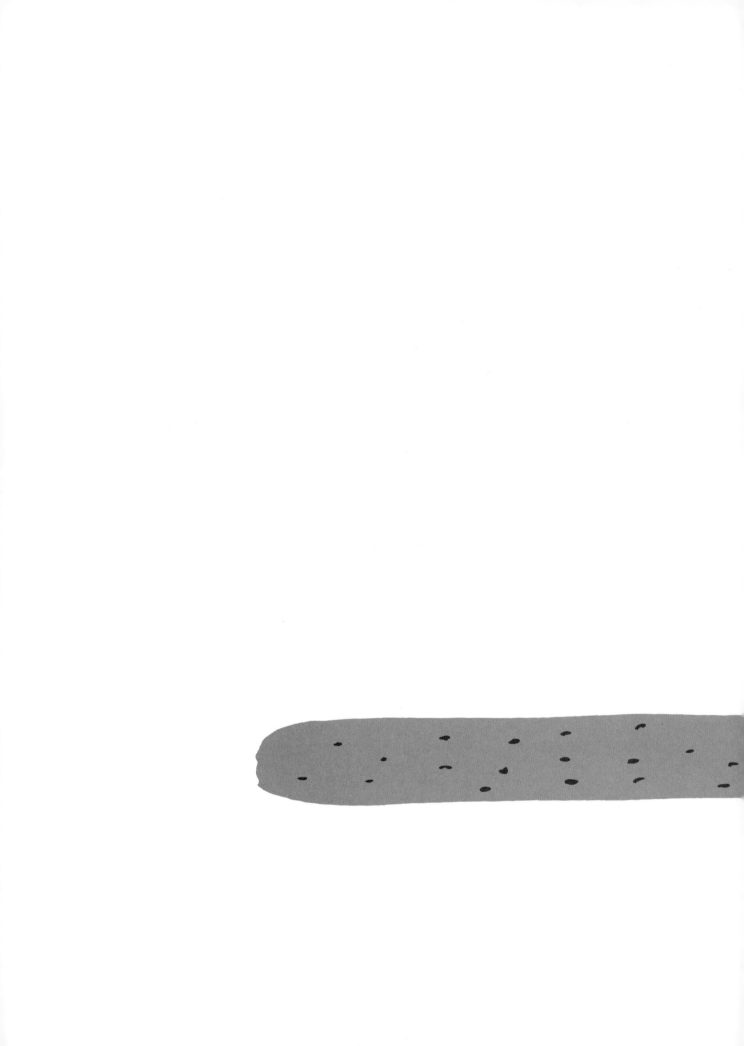

YOU WERE A BABY ONCE.

EVERYONE WAS A BABY ONCE.

BUT HOW DO YOU MAKE A BABY?

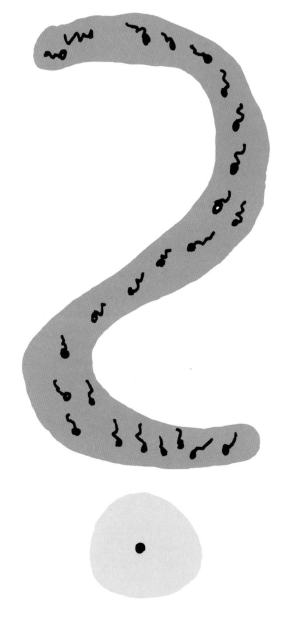

WITH DANGEROUS CHEMICALS?

DO STORKS BRING BABIES?

WITH BUTTER, SUGAR, FLOUR AND EGGS?

FROM CLAY?

HAMMER AND NAILS?

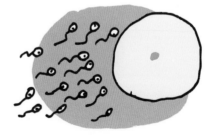

WITH SPERM AND AN EGG?

MAKING A BABY BEGINS WITH LOVE.
THERE ARE MANY KINDS OF LOVE.

WE LOVE EACH OTHER IN OUR FAMILY.

I LOVE BEING
WITH MY FRIEND.   ME TOO!

I LOVE MY
CUDDLY TOY.

I LOVE
MY DOG.

WE'RE
A COUPLE.   WE LOVE
EACH OTHER.

COUPLES IN LOVE WANT TO BE TOGETHER ALL THE TIME.

TO ENJOY THINGS TOGETHER.

EAT TOGETHER.

TALK AND GET TO KNOW EACH OTHER.

TO SIT VERY, VERY CLOSE.

PEOPLE IN LOVE ENJOY BEING
AS CLOSE AS POSSIBLE.

THEY HUG, KISS AND TOUCH EACH OTHER.

TO GET EVEN CLOSER THEY TAKE OFF
THEIR CLOTHES AND HUG.

WHEN PAPA'S PENIS IS IN MAMA'S VAGINA
THEY'RE AS CLOSE AS TWO PEOPLE CAN BE.

CUDDLING TOGETHER NAKED, MAN AND WOMAN, WOMAN AND WOMAN,
OR MAN AND MAN IS CALLED HAVING SEX. IT'S SOMETHING ADULT
COUPLES DO BECAUSE THEY LIKE IT.

HAVING SEX IS ALSO CALLED MAKING LOVE OR HAVING INTERCOURSE. WHO IS HAVING SEX HERE?

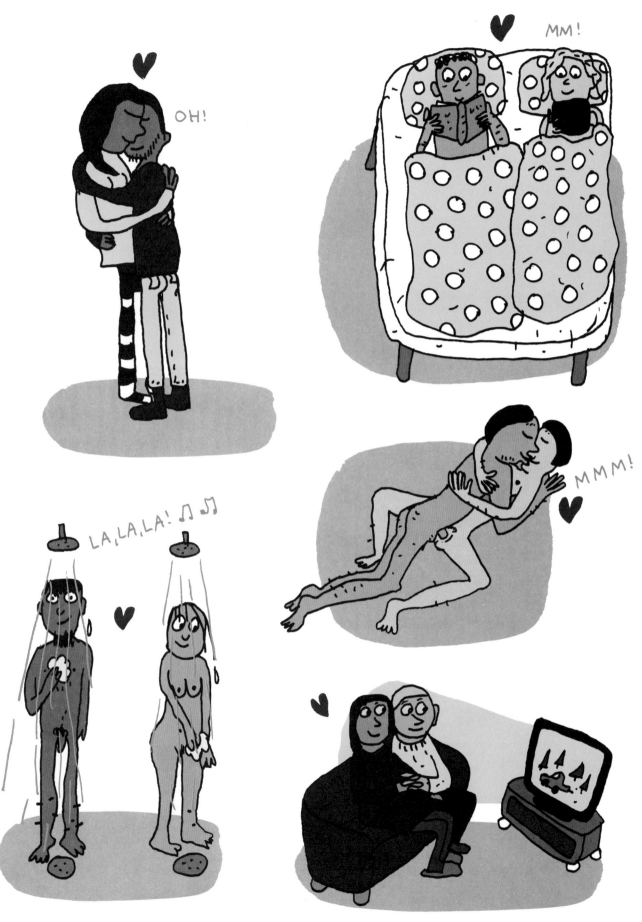

MWAH!

LOVELY!

OOOHH!

HA, HA!

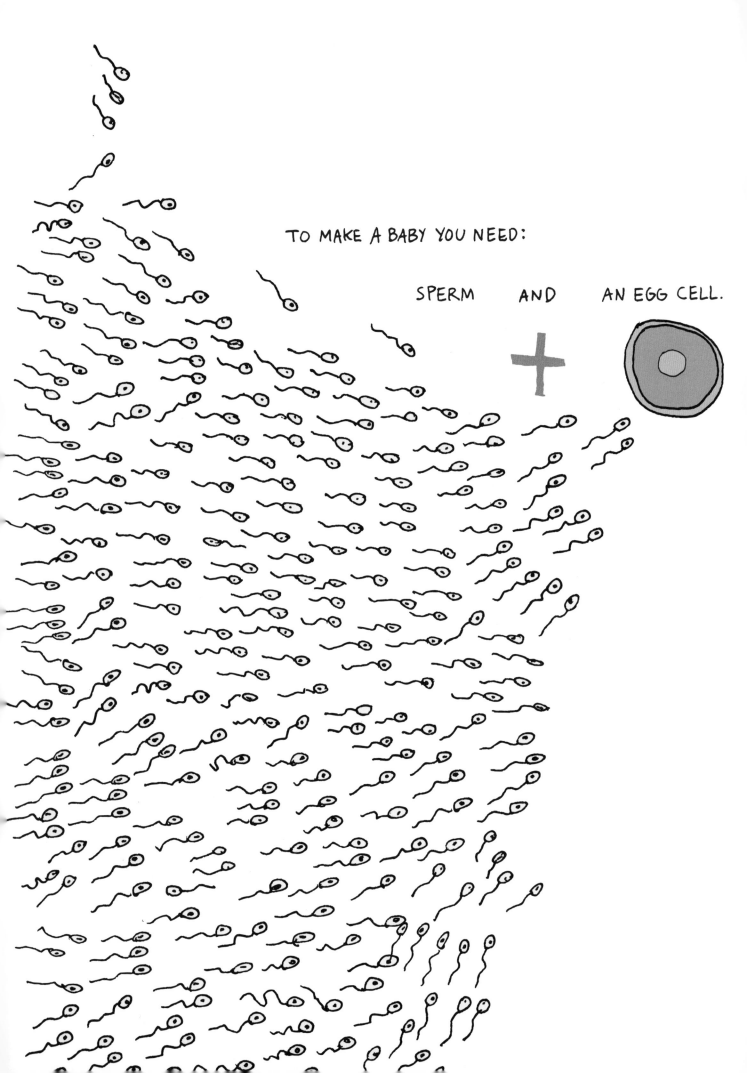

TO MAKE A BABY YOU NEED:

SPERM AND AN EGG CELL.

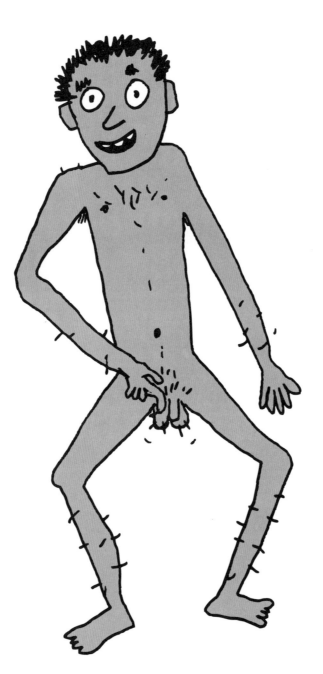

SPERM ARE MADE INSIDE A MAN'S TESTICLES.

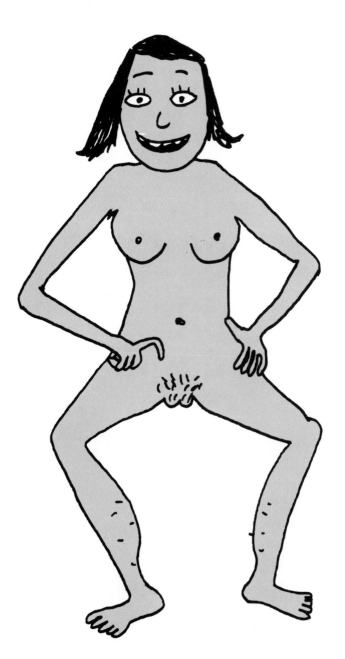

EGGS ARE MADE INSIDE A WOMAN'S OVARIES.

WHEN A WOMAN AND A MAN HAVE SEX WITH THE PENIS IN THE VAGINA, SPERM ARE RELEASED FROM THE PENIS AND MILLIONS OF THEM SWIM TO THE EGG IN THE OVARY.

MAYBE THIS WILL BECOME A BABY!

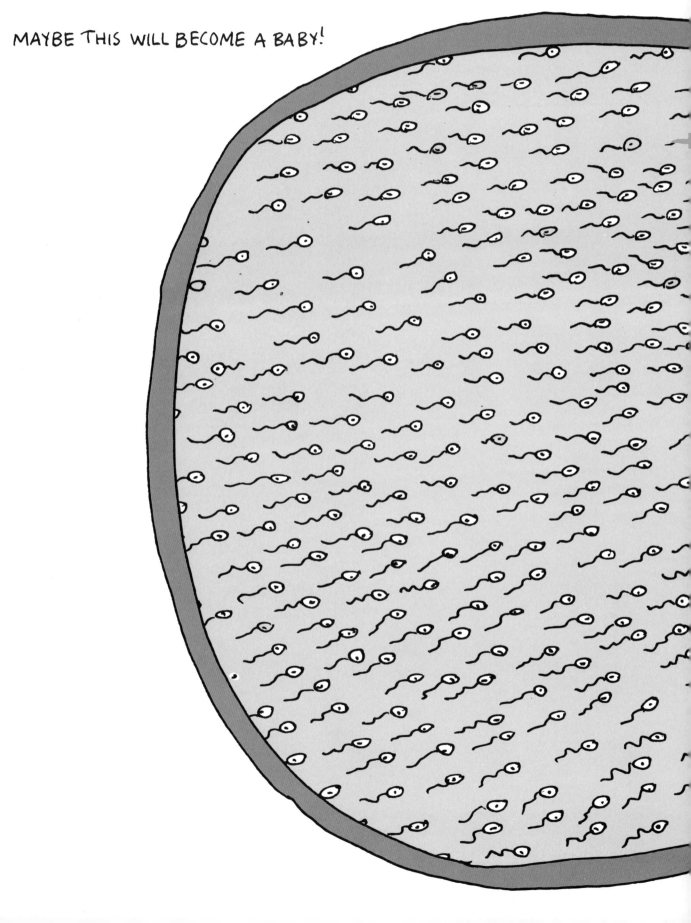

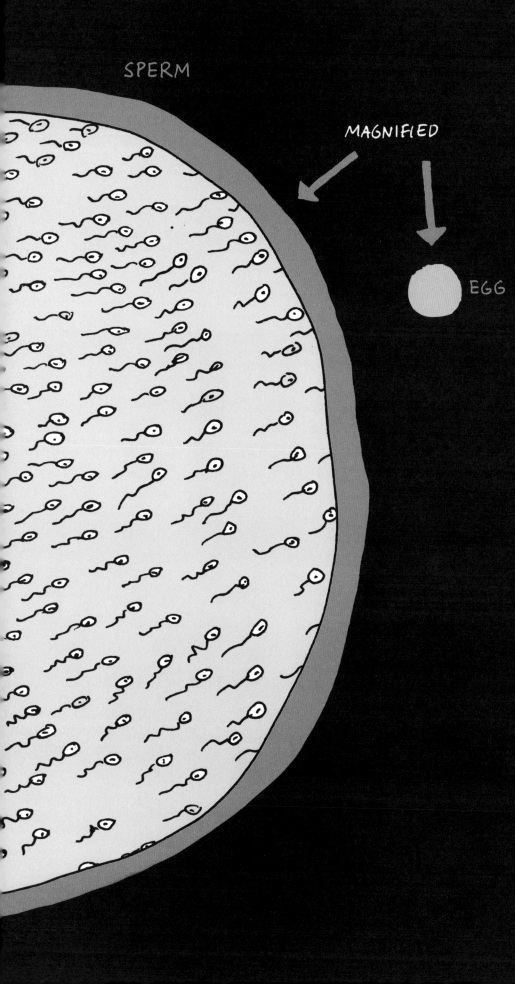

THE EGG IS AS SMALL AS A TINY, WEENY DOT,
AND THE SPERM ARE SO SMALL
THEY'RE IMPOSSIBLE TO SEE.

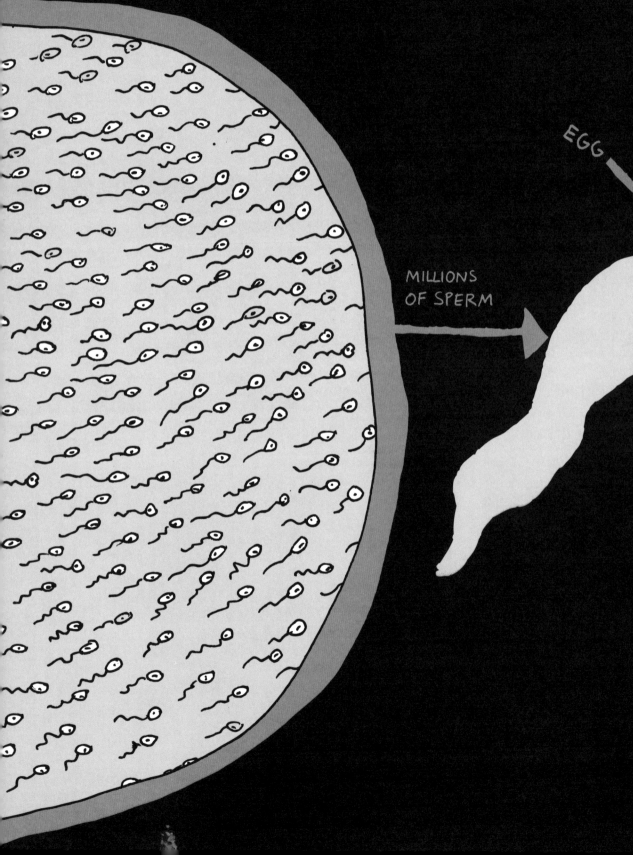

EGG

MILLIONS
OF SPERM

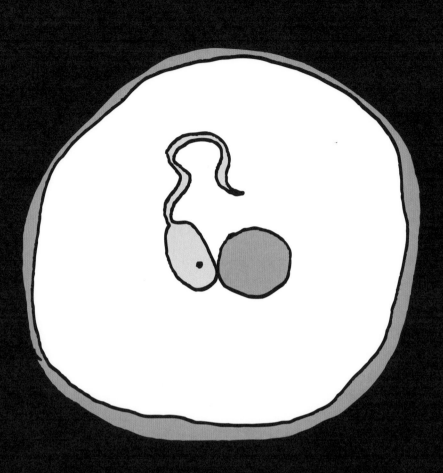

WHEN A SPERM AND AN EGG JOIN, THE EGG IS FERTILIZED
AND CAN GROW INTO AN EMBRYO, A BABY.

THIS HAPPENS IN THE UTERUS, A SPECIAL SAFE PLACE
INSIDE A WOMAN'S BODY.

SOMETIMES THE EGG SPLITS INTO TWO, SO TWO BABIES
ARE MADE—TWINS! TWINS CAN ALSO BE MADE IF THERE
ARE TWO EGGS. TWINS ARE QUITE RARE.

SOME COUPLES CAN'T MAKE BABIES
WHEN THEY HAVE SEX.

I DON'T HAVE
ENOUGH SPERM.

WE DON'T HAVE
ANY SPERM.

MY EGGS CAN'T
BE FERTILIZED.

BUT THERE ARE WAYS TO HELP THE SPERM AND
EGG JOIN, USING A SYRINGE OR IN A TEST TUBE.

THE SYRINGE SQUIRTS SPERM INTO THE UTERUS,
WHERE THEY MEET THE EGG.

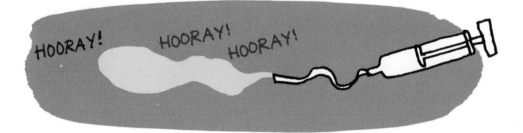

YOU CAN REMOVE THE EGG AND SPERM AND
COMBINE THEM IN A TEST TUBE OR DISH,
THEN RETURN THEM TO THE UTERUS.

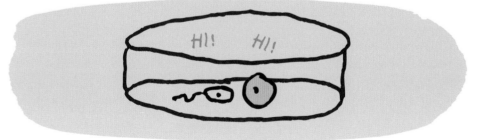

THE USUAL WAY TO MAKE A BABY IS BY SEXUAL INTERCOURSE BETWEEN A MAN AND A WOMAN.

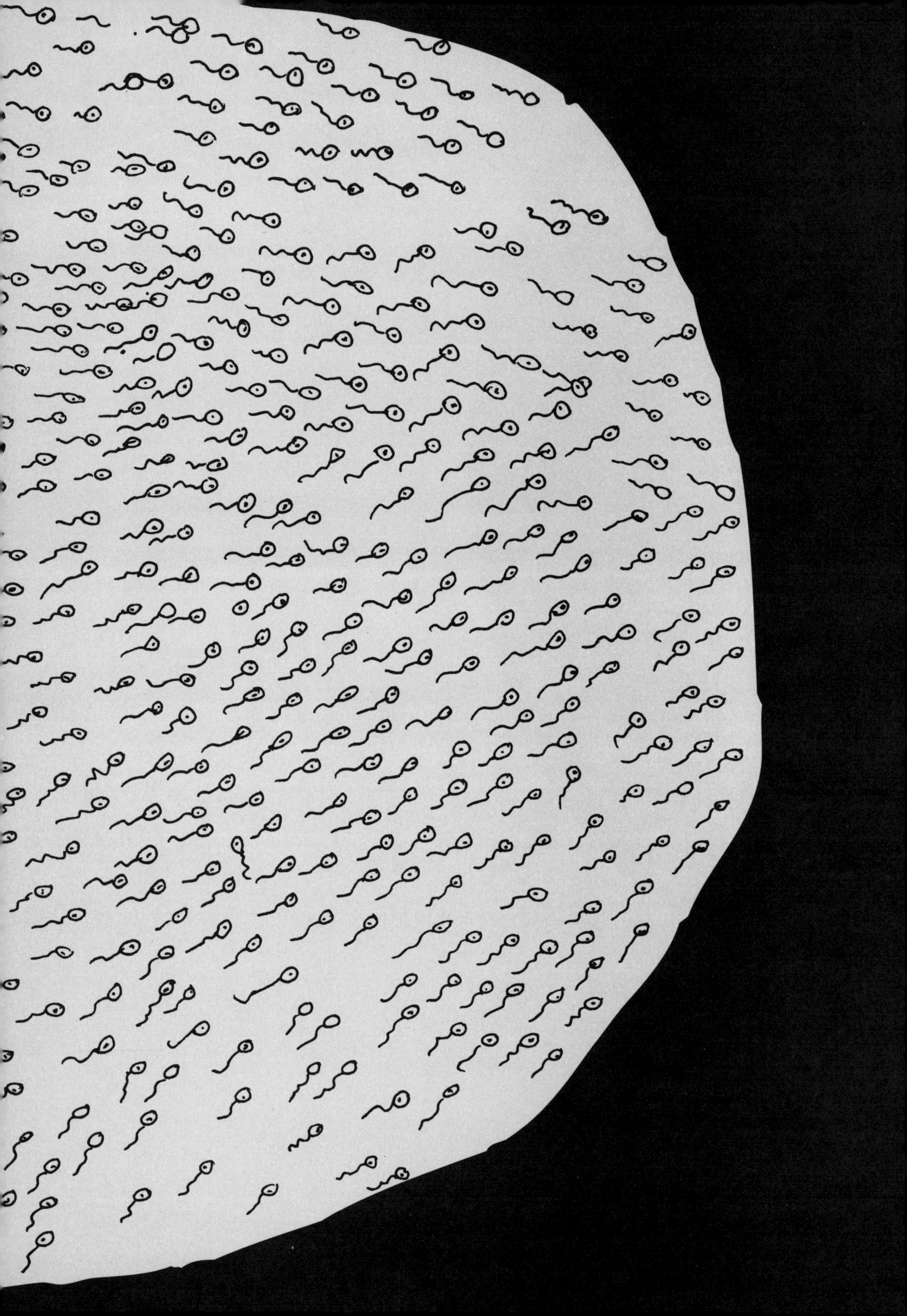

NOW THE SPERM ARE ON THEIR WAY TO THE EGG.
SWIM FOR YOUR LIFE!

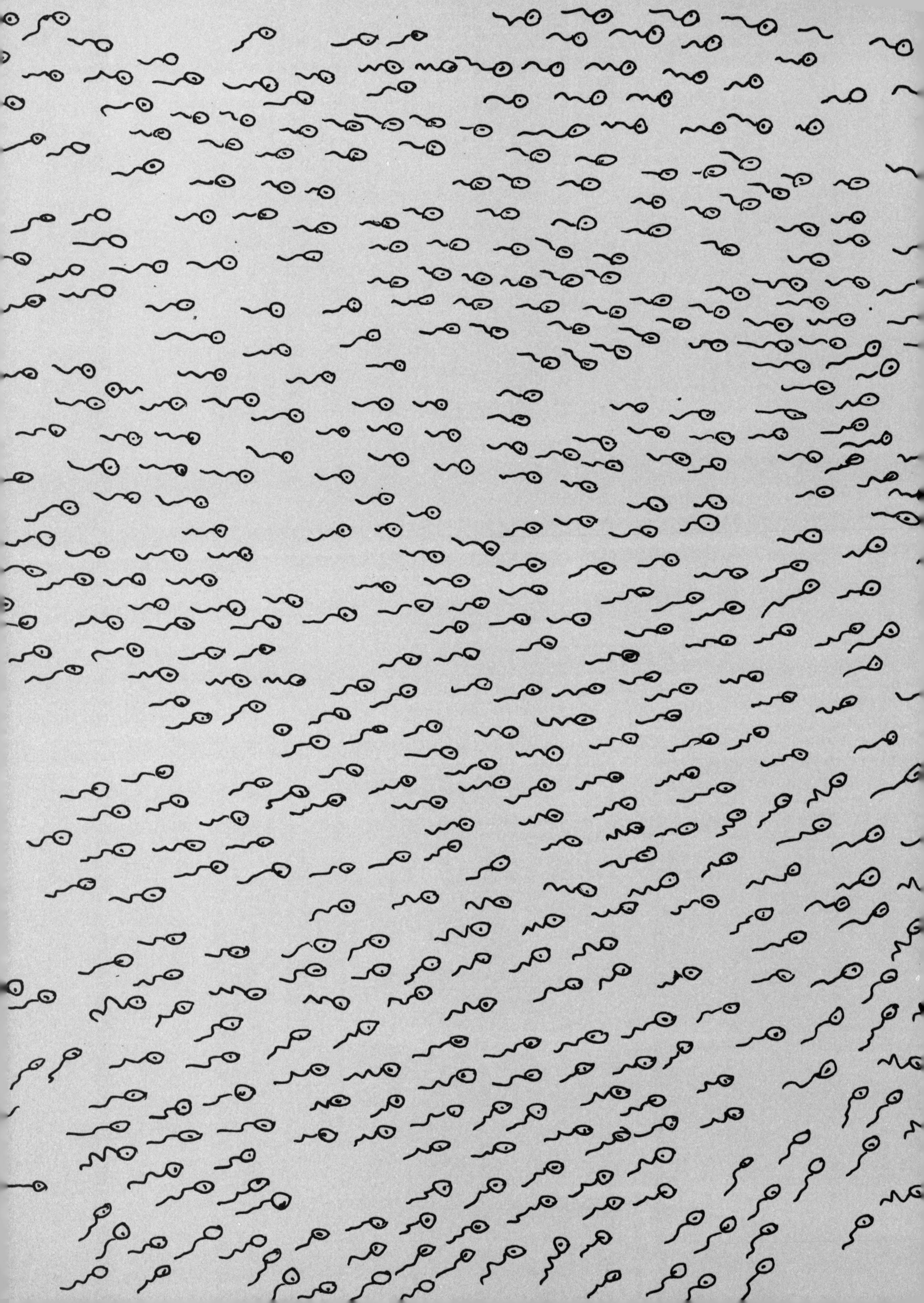

I'M THE FASTEST!

I WANT TO WIN!

HMM, WHICH ONE
SHALL I CHOOSE?

I'M WINNING!

HI, EGGIE!

LOOK OUT!

CHOOSE ME!

MOVE OVER!

I'M THE ONE!

OUT OF MY WAY!

I'M WINNING!

HERE I COME!

PICK ME!

I'M FASTEST!

WATCH OUT!

CHOOSE ME!

I WANT TO BE THE ONE!

LET ME PAST! I'M WINNING!

I'M WINNING!

THE EGG WILL ONLY TAKE ONE.
WHICH ONE DO YOU THINK IT WILL BE?

MAYBE NONE OF THEM WILL
GET THERE THIS TIME.

ONLY A FEW OF THE SPERM MANAGE TO SWIM
ALL THE WAY TO THE EGG.

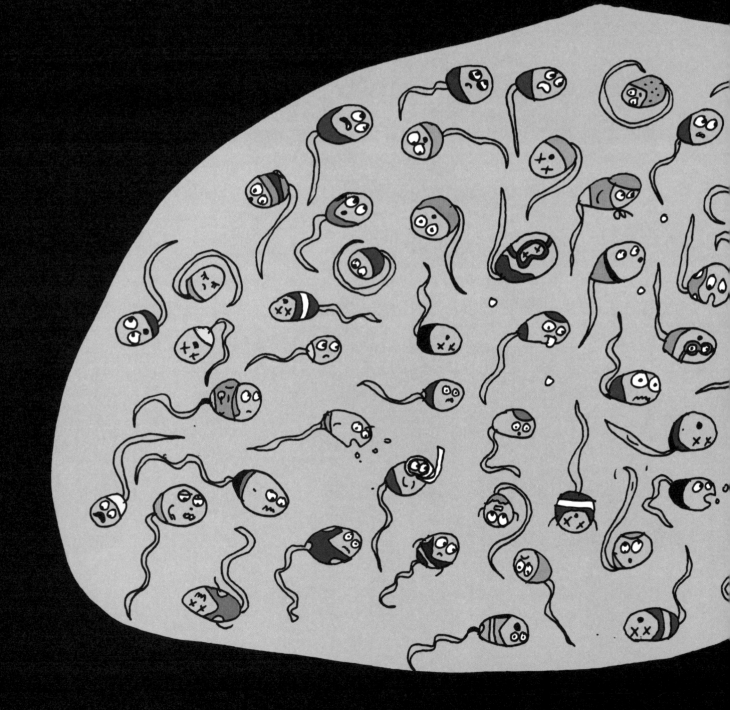

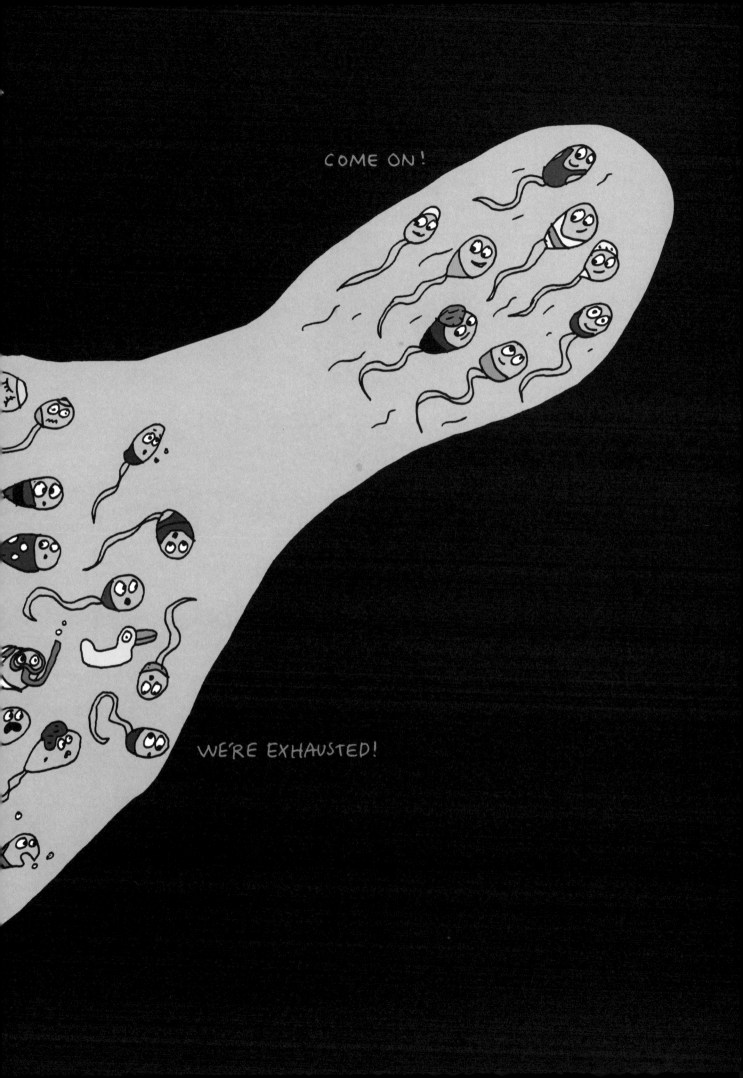

SOME PEOPLE MAKE A BABY THE FIRST TIME THEY TRY.
SOMETIMES IT TAKES MANY TRIES AND A LONG TIME.

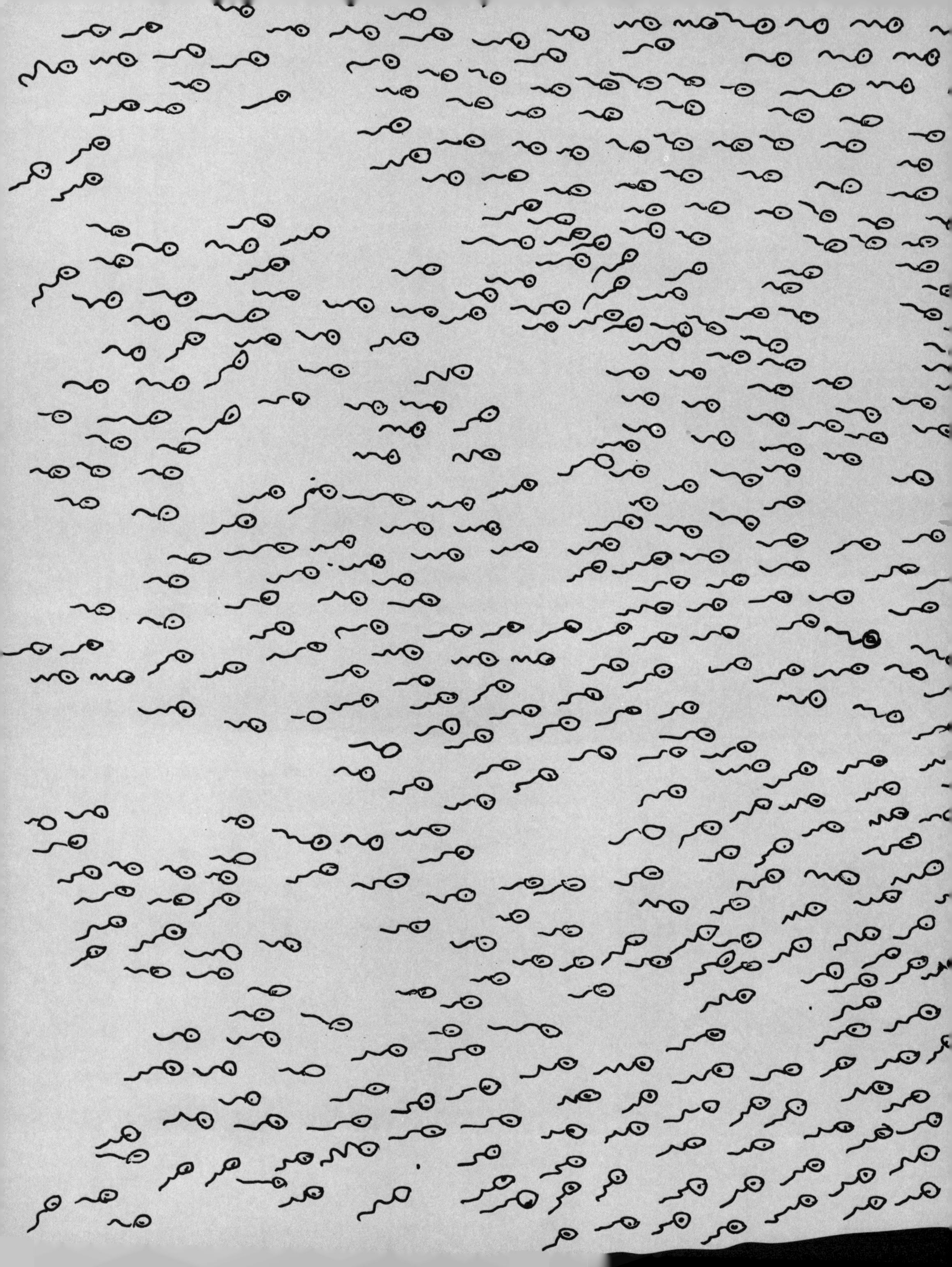

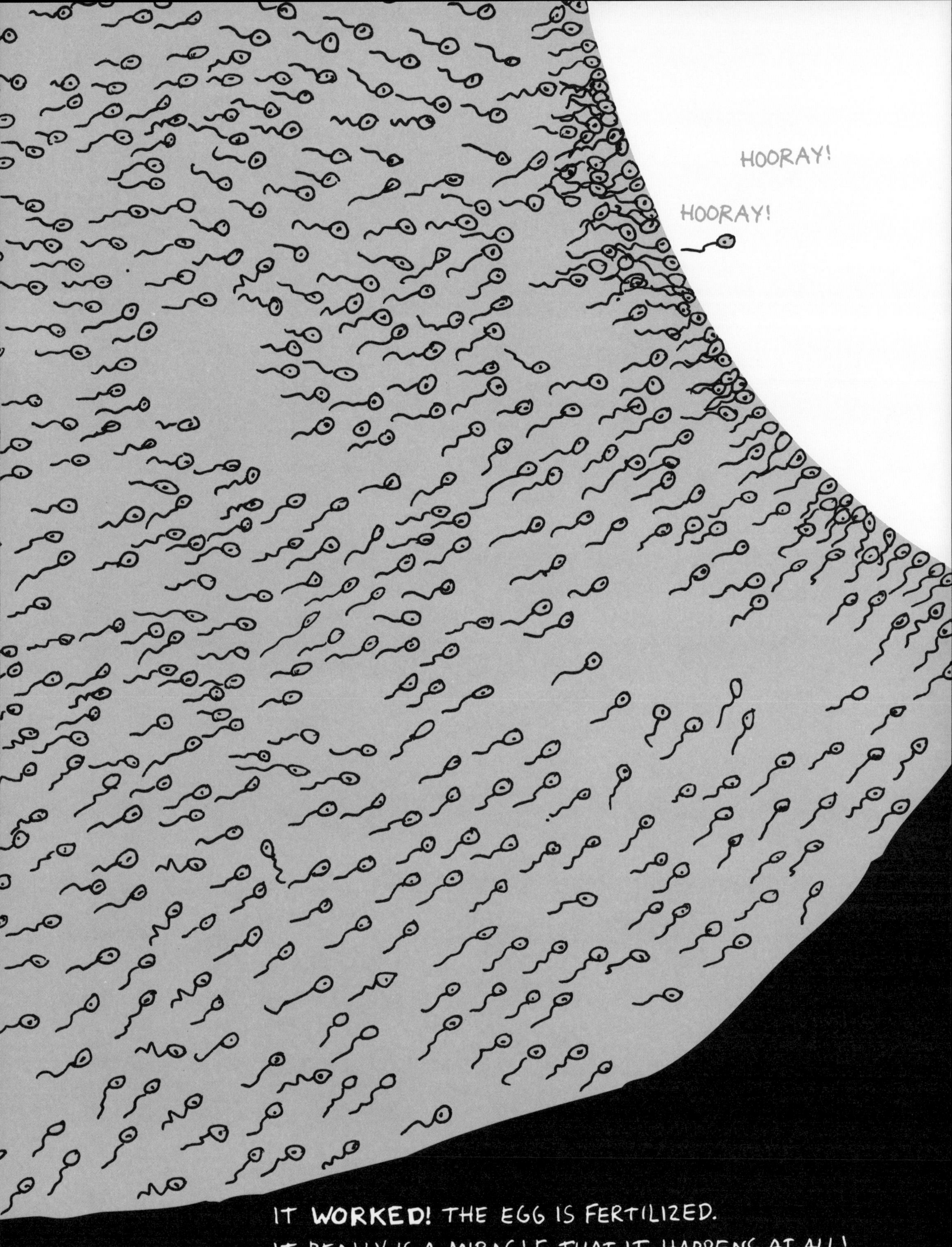

IT **WORKED!** THE EGG IS FERTILIZED.
IT REALLY IS A MIRACLE THAT IT HAPPENS AT ALL!
YOU'RE A MIRACLE!

WHEN THE SPERM IS IN THE EGG, THE EGG CLOSES UP
SO NO OTHER SPERM CAN GET IN.

THE SPERM DETERMINES WHETHER IT WILL BE
A GIRL OR A BOY.

THE SPERM LOSES ITS TAIL AND TOGETHER THE EGG
AND THE SPERM FORM A CELL, WHICH DIVIDES...

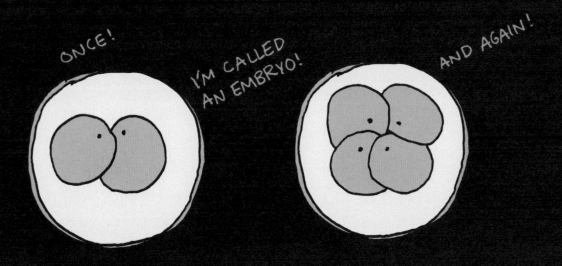

ONCE!

I'M CALLED
AN EMBRYO!

AND AGAIN!

AND DIVIDES...

AGAIN!

AND AGAIN!

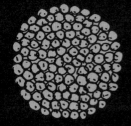

AND THE EMBRYO GROWS BIGGER
AND BIGGER.

THIS IS GOING TO BE A BABY. IMAGINE THAT!

AS THE FERTILIZED EGG DIVIDES, IT TRAVELS DOWN THE
FALLOPIAN TUBE TO THE UTERUS, WHERE IT SETTLES IN.

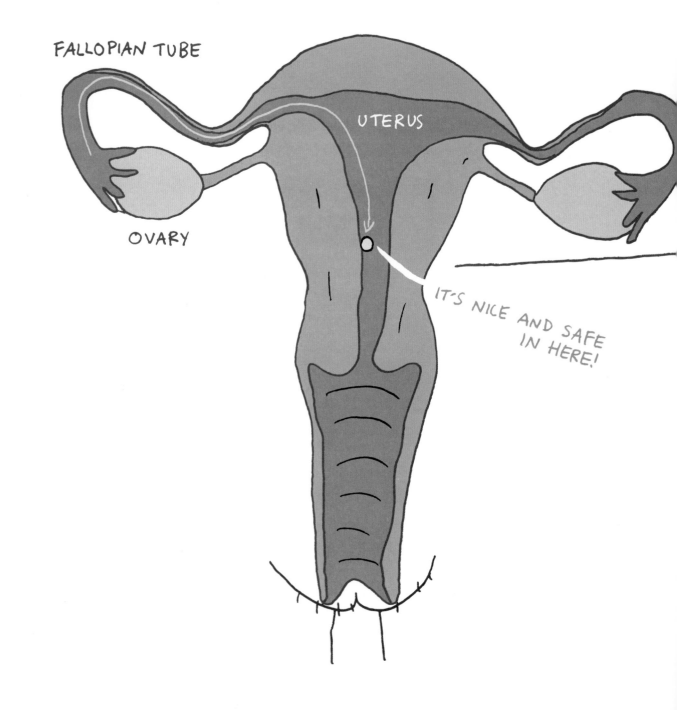

FALLOPIAN TUBE

UTERUS

OVARY

IT'S NICE AND SAFE
IN HERE!

THE EMBRYO KEEPS GROWING IN THE UTERUS.

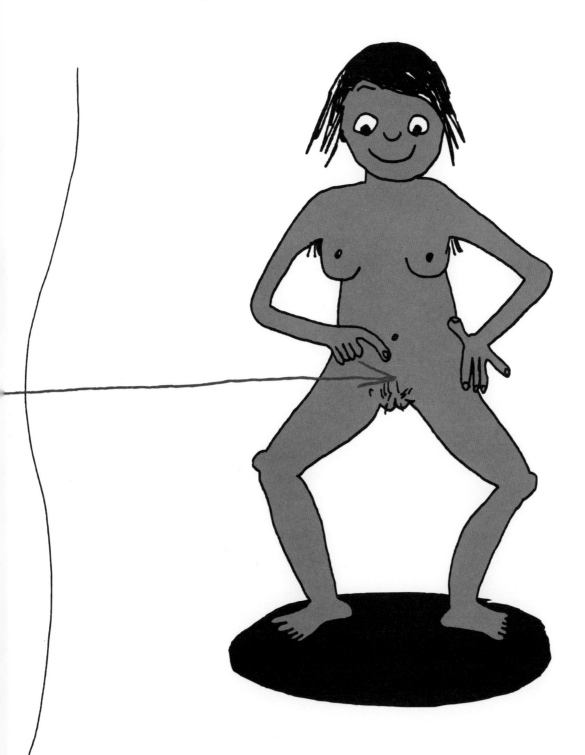

AFTER A FEW WEEKS THE CELLS HAVE BECOME
A TINY BODY.

THIS IS HOW TEENY-TINY I AM!

JUST THINK, ONCE WE WERE ALL
AS TINY AS THAT.

AFTER A FEW MORE WEEKS THE CELLS
ARE BECOMING A BABY.

HOORAY!

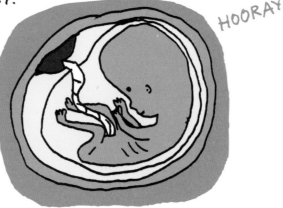

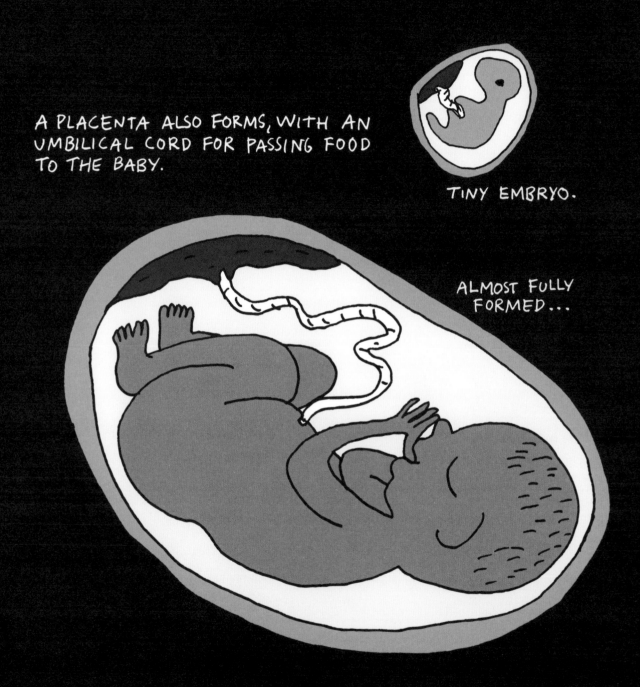

A PLACENTA ALSO FORMS, WITH AN UMBILICAL CORD FOR PASSING FOOD TO THE BABY.

TINY EMBRYO.

ALMOST FULLY FORMED...

ENERGY FROM FOOD GOES FIRST INTO THE MOTHER'S BLOOD, THEN THROUGH THE PLACENTA AND UMBILICAL CORD TO THE GROWING BABY.

THE DEVELOPING BABY IS SURROUNDED BY LIQUID CALLED AMNIOTIC FLUID.

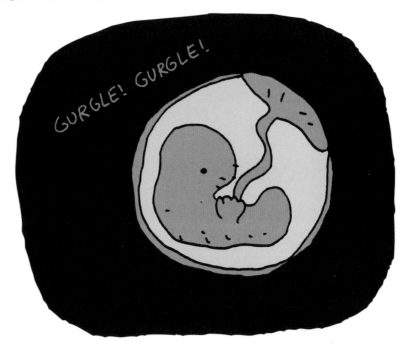

WE'RE BOTH ALL WET! ME IN MY BATH AND YOU IN YOUR AMNIOTIC FLUID.

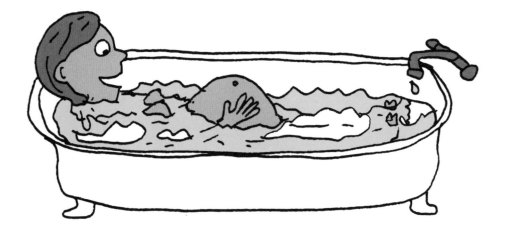

THE BABY DOESN'T NEED TO BREATHE. WE GET OXYGEN BY BREATHING AIR. THE BABY GETS IT THROUGH THE UMBILICAL CORD FROM THEIR MOTHER'S BLOOD.

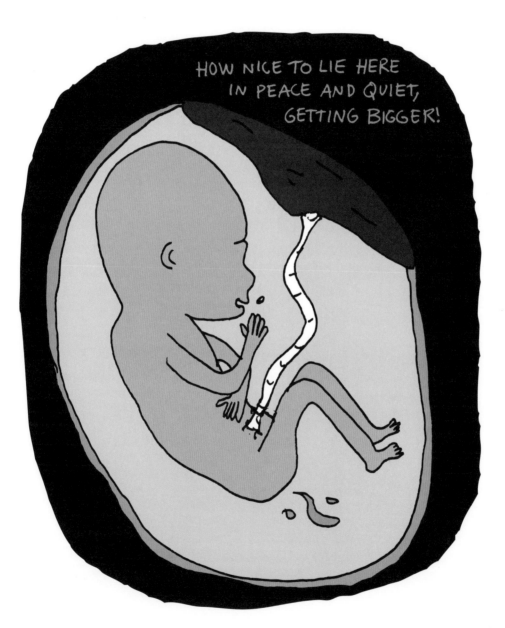

THE BABY DRINKS THE FLUID AND PEES IT OUT.
THE FLUID IS BEING MADE FRESH AND NEW ALL THE TIME.

THE MOTHER CAN FEEL VERY TIRED AND
SICK WHEN SHE FIRST GETS PREGNANT.

YAWN!

HER BODY IS GETTING READY TO LOOK AFTER THE BABY.

I'M FINE, MAMA!

THE MOTHER MIGHT NOT EAT SO MUCH IF SHE'S FEELING SICK,
BUT THE BABY'S GETTING ALL THE NUTRITION THEY NEED.

EVERY MINUTE, EVERY DAY, EVERY MONTH THE BABY IS GROWING IN THE UTERUS.

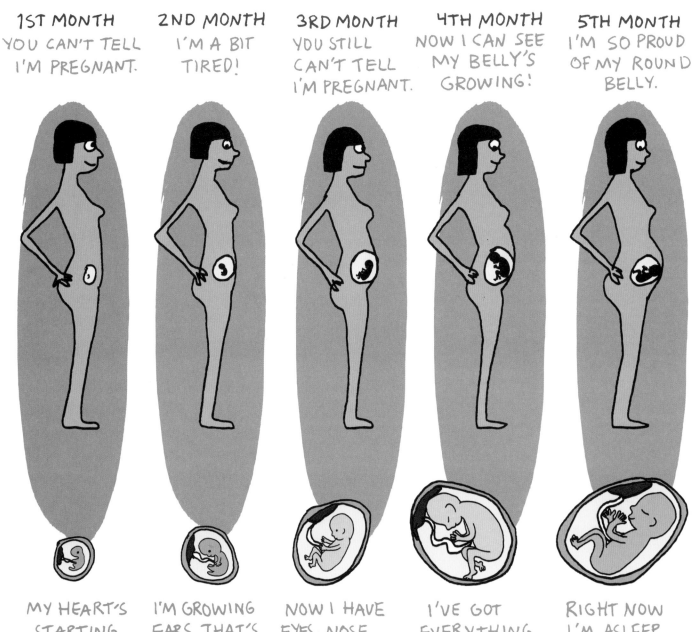

1ST MONTH
YOU CAN'T TELL I'M PREGNANT.

2ND MONTH
I'M A BIT TIRED!

3RD MONTH
YOU STILL CAN'T TELL I'M PREGNANT.

4TH MONTH
NOW I CAN SEE MY BELLY'S GROWING!

5TH MONTH
I'M SO PROUD OF MY ROUND BELLY.

MY HEART'S STARTING TO BEAT.

I'M GROWING EARS. THAT'S CLEVER.

NOW I HAVE EYES, NOSE, MOUTH, ARMS AND LEGS. THAT'S COOL!

I'VE GOT EVERYTHING I NEED.

RIGHT NOW I'M ASLEEP.

THE MAMA'S BELLY GETS BIGGER AND BIGGER,
MAKING ROOM FOR THE BABY.

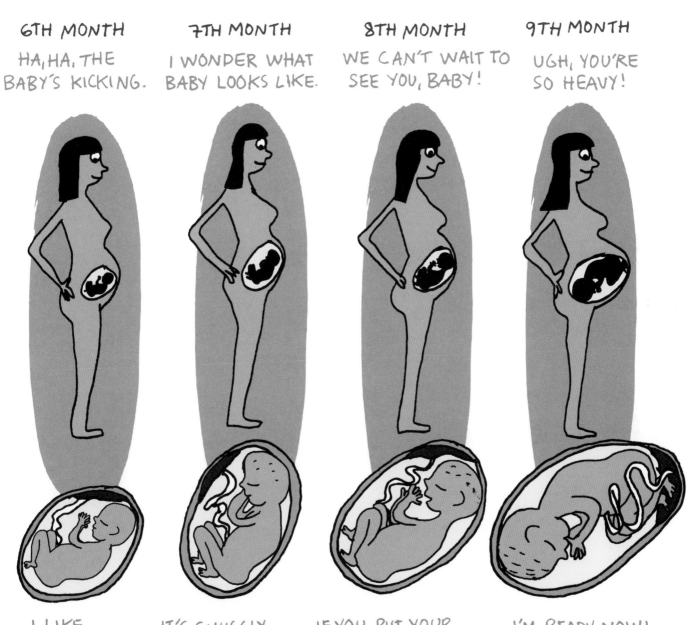

6TH MONTH
HA, HA, THE
BABY'S KICKING.

7TH MONTH
I WONDER WHAT
BABY LOOKS LIKE.

8TH MONTH
WE CAN'T WAIT TO
SEE YOU, BABY!

9TH MONTH
UGH, YOU'RE
SO HEAVY!

I LIKE
WRIGGLING
AROUND.

IT'S SNUGGLY
IN HERE!

IF YOU PUT YOUR
EAR TO MAMA'S
BELLY YOU CAN
HEAR MY HEART
BEATING.

I'M READY NOW!

PREGNANT MOTHERS ALL LOOK DIFFERENT.

MY BELLY'S BIG,
BUT NOT GIGANTIC.

NOT PREGNANT   PREGNANT

I'M SO PROUD OF
MY PREGNANT BELLY.

THE PARENTS RUSH AROUND PREPARING FOR THE NEW BABY.

A HUNDRED BIBS. WILL THAT DO?

SURELY!

IMAGINE, OUR BABY WILL BE LYING HERE!

THEY WAIT AND WAIT AND WAIT.

THEY IMAGINE HOW IT WILL BE
AND WHAT THE BABY WILL LOOK LIKE.

TIME PASSES VERY SLOWLY WHEN YOU'RE WAITING FOR A BABY.

AFTER ABOUT NINE MONTHS THE BABY IS READY
AND WANTS TO COME OUT.

IT'S NOT ALWAYS EASY TO KNOW WHEN IT'S TIME.
THE PARENTS PHONE THEIR MIDWIFE OR DOCTOR TO ASK.

DOCTORS AND MIDWIVES KNOW ALL ABOUT
HOW BABIES ARE BORN.

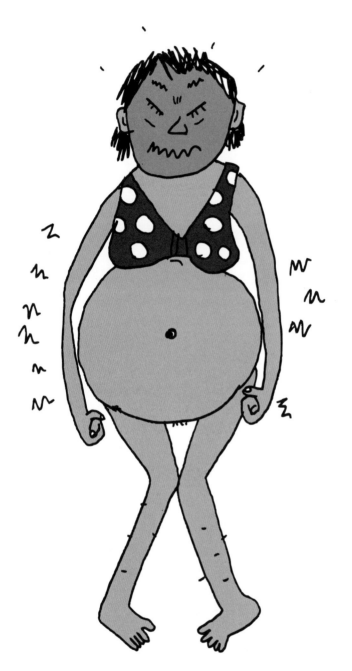

MUSCLES AROUND THE MOTHER'S UTERUS START
SQUEEZING TO PUSH THE BABY OUT.

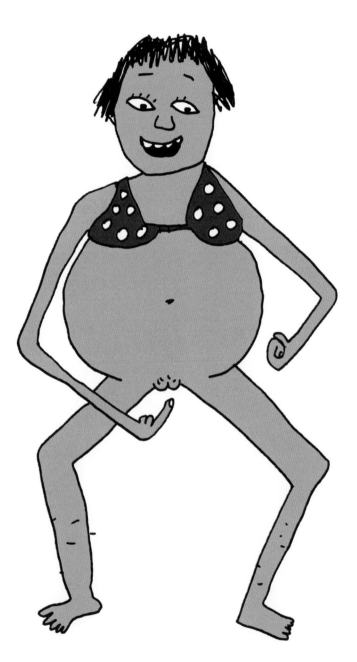

THE BABY WILL BE BORN THROUGH THE VAGINA.

GIVING BIRTH IS HARD WORK, BUT MAMA'S TOUGH.
SHE'S VERY STRONG.

GREAT WORK, DARLING!

YOU'RE AMAZING!

ALL BIRTHS ARE DIFFERENT. SOME BABIES CAN'T WAIT
TO GET OUT. OTHERS TAKE THEIR TIME.

SOMETIMES THE BABY WON'T OR CAN'T
COME OUT THROUGH THE VAGINA.
THEN IT IS BORN BY CAESAREAN SECTION.

THE BABY IS REMOVED FROM THE UTERUS
THROUGH A CUT IN THE MOTHER'S BELLY.

THE UMBILICAL CORD THAT FED THE BABY IS CUT.

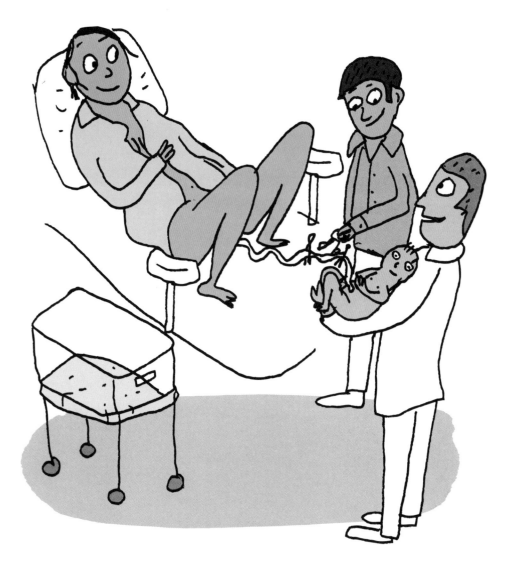

THE MOTHER PUSHES OUT THE PLACENTA AS WELL.

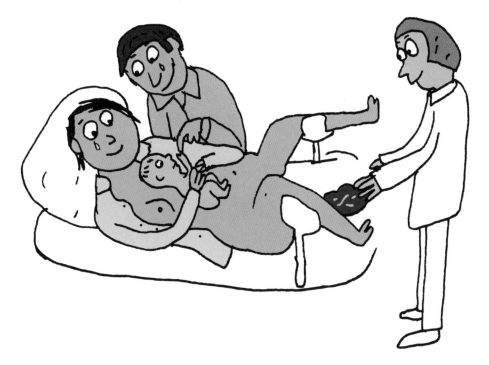

THE PLACENTA LOOKS A BIT LIKE A SMALL TREE,
WITH THE UMBILICAL CORD FOR A TRUNK.
SOME PEOPLE CALL IT THE TREE OF LIFE.

THE PARENTS ARE FILLED WITH LOVE FOR
THEIR NEW BABY, AND THEY LOOK FORWARD
TO WATCHING IT GROW.

NOW THEY ARE A FAMILY.

OR AN EVEN BIGGER FAMILY.

CHILDREN BORN TO PARENTS WHO CAN'T LOOK
AFTER THEM CAN BE ADOPTED.

PARENTS WHO ADOPT A CHILD HAVE BEEN WAITING
FOR A VERY, VERY, VERY LONG TIME.

OUR BABY!

LOTS AND LOTS OF BABIES ARE BORN
ALL OVER THE WORLD EVERY DAY.

A NEW BABY IN THE WORLD IS ONE OF
THE MOST BRILLIANT AND BEAUTIFUL
THINGS THERE IS.

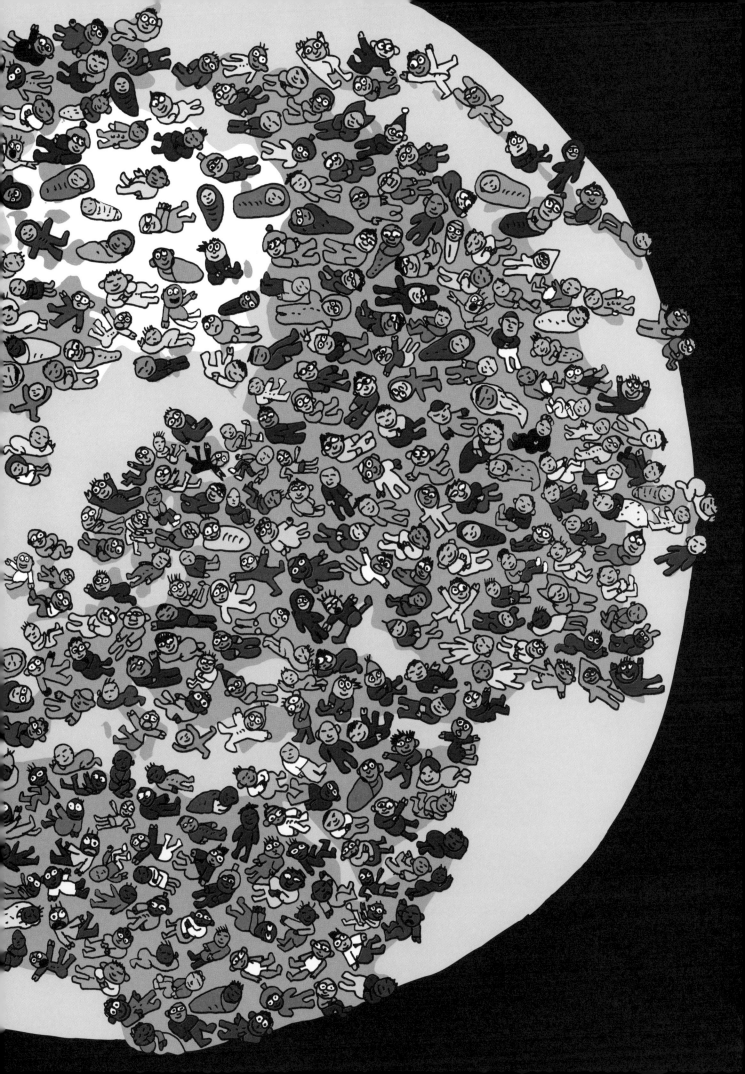

EVERY CHILD IS DIFFERENT. THERE'S ONLY ONE LIKE YOU.
IT'S A MIRACLE THAT WE ARE BORN AND EXIST.
IT'S A MIRACLE AND SO PERFECT THAT YOU ARE YOU.

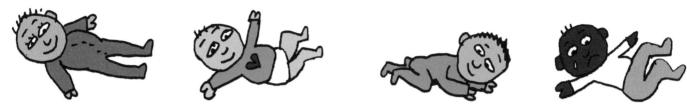